MORE POTATOES!
by Millicent E. Selsam
Pictures by Ben Shecter

A Science I CAN READ Book

Harper & Row, Publishers
New York, Evanston, San Francisco, London

MORE POTATOES!
Text copyright © 1972 by Millicent E. Selsam
Pictures copyright © 1972 by Ben Shecter

Trade Standard Book Number: 06-025323-I
Harpercrest Standard Book Number: 06-025324-X
Library of Congress Catalog Card Number: 78-183167
FIRST EDITION

In memory of George C. Bartilucci

Sue watched her mother peel potatoes.

"How are you making the potatoes

tonight?" she asked.

"I am not making the potatoes.

I am only cooking them, Sue.

But I have no more potatoes.

Will you get some for me?"

asked her mother.

Sue went to the store

and found the vegetable man.

"May I have two pounds

of potatoes, please?" she said.

"Here," said the man.

"You are taking

my last two pounds.

I have no more potatoes."

"How are you going to get more?"

asked Sue.

"Don't bother me,"

said the vegetable man.

"I am busy."

Sue ran home

to give her mother the potatoes.

In a few minutes

she was back at the store.

The vegetable man

was writing

on a big sheet of paper.

Oranges
Potatoes
Lettuce

"Hi," said Sue.

"You again?" he said.

"Won't you tell me

how you get more potatoes?"

asked Sue.

"All right. Come closer.

Look at this.

Do you see the word *potatoes*?

10

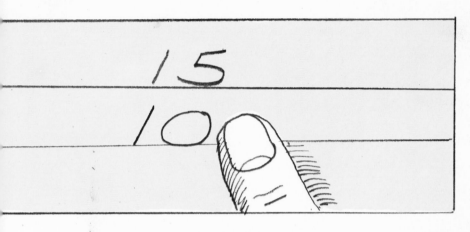

Next to the word *potatoes*," he said,

"I am writing the number of bags

I need for tomorrow."

"How many do you need?"

asked Sue.

"Ten bags.

That's five hundred pounds,"

said the vegetable man.

"That's a lot of potatoes," said Sue.

"Where do they come from?"

The vegetable man said,

"From our warehouse.

The same one that sends

all my vegetables.

I am going to call them now."

Sue listened to the vegetable man

give his order.

She heard him say,

"five hundred pounds."

"That must be the potatoes,"

said Sue.

The vegetable man hung up.

13

Sue asked him, "When does

the warehouse send the vegetables?"

"The truck will be here

at seven o'clock

tomorrow morning.

You will be asleep,"

said the vegetable man.

"Oh no," said Sue. "I will be here."

The next morning

Sue woke before seven o'clock.

She went down to the store.

The truck was there!

On the sidewalk

there were bags and boxes.

She found some bags

that had the word

potatoes on them.

Just then, the vegetable man

walked out of the store.

"Oh, you again!" he said.

"Your potatoes are here

from the warehouse. May I go

to that warehouse?" said Sue.

The vegetable man looked at Sue.

"Well, maybe. Ask your mother

to write a letter," he said.

"Where?" asked Sue.

"Come inside,"

said the vegetable man.

"I will give you the address."

Sue gave the address to her mother.

"I don't think they will let you

go alone," her mother said.

"But they might let your class go."

That day at school,

Sue asked her teacher,

"Can the class go

to see the warehouse?"

"What warehouse?" asked the teacher.

"Well," said Sue,

"my mother needed potatoes.

I went to the store to get them.

The vegetable man gave me

his last two pounds.

"So I asked him where he was going

to get more potatoes.

He said that a truck brings

the potatoes from the warehouse.

This morning I saw the truck

in front of the store.

I saw the bags of potatoes.

Now I want to go to the warehouse.

My mother said to ask you

if the class can go.

Here is the address

of the warehouse.

Can we go?"

The teacher said to the class,

"You heard the story.

How many of you

want to visit this warehouse?"

They all raised their hands.

Sue's teacher wrote a letter

to the warehouse.

Nothing happened

for a week.

Then a letter came.

It said, "Your class may come

to the warehouse any day

between eleven and twelve o'clock."

It was signed "J. Green."

The next Monday, the class rode

to the warehouse.

Mr. Green met them.

He showed them

trucks being loaded

with potatoes and other vegetables.

"Where do the trucks go?"

asked one of the children.

"I know," said Sue.

"They go to the stores,"

"That is right," said Mr. Green.

"These trucks take the food

to our stores all over the city."

24

Then Mr. Green showed them

where railroad cars and trucks

bring in the vegetables.

"Some cars and trucks are filled

with bags of potatoes," he said.

"But where do the potatoes

come from?" asked Sue.

"From farms," said Mr. Green.

"May I take these children

to a potato farm?"

asked the teacher.

"Well," said Mr. Green.

"You can try Mr. Bartilucci's farm.

It is not too far from the city."

The next day at school,

the teacher wrote to Mr. Bartilucci.

About a week later,

the teacher said,

"We can visit Mr. Bartilucci's

potato farm next Tuesday."

On Tuesday,

the class rode out to the farm.

Mr. Bartilucci was waiting for them.

The teacher said to him,

"We would like to see

how you grow potatoes."

28

"The potatoes are already

in the ground," said Mr. Bartilucci.

"You mean we are too late?"

asked Sue.

"No, but the potato plants

are already growing.

I planted them in May.

Now it is June."

"Do you plant them from seeds?"

asked the teacher.

"No," said Mr. Bartilucci.

"We plant small potatoes.

We call them *seed* potatoes."

He took a seed potato

from his pocket.

He cut the potato

in half.

Then he cut each half across.

He had four pieces.

"These are the pieces

of potato we plant.

Each piece must have

at least one or two eyes.

The eyes are the places on the potato

where the buds are.

New potato plants grow

from these buds."

"How do you plant them?"

asked one of the boys.

"Do you go along and drop them

in the ground?"

"Oh no," said Mr. Bartilucci.

"The farm is too big for that.

I have a machine

that plants the potatoes,"

He took the class to the barn

to show them the machine.

"This machine plants

two rows of potatoes at a time."

Mr. Bartilucci showed them

two sharp wheels

in the front.

"These wheels dig the rows,"

he said.

Then he showed them

two empty metal boxes

at the back of the machine.

"In the bottom of each box

is a wheel with spikes.

As the wheel turns, the spikes

pick up the potatoes.

Then they drop them to the ground,

one by one.

And here are two more sharp wheels.

These cover the potatoes with soil,"

he said.

"Do you want to see
what the potato plants
look like now?"
asked Mr. Bartilucci.
"Then follow me."

The class followed Mr. Bartilucci
to his fields.
As far as they could see,
there were rows of green plants.

There were white flowers

on the plants.

"I see the plants," said Sue.

"But where are the potatoes?"

Mr. Bartilucci took a shovel
and dug under one plant.
Then he lifted the whole plant
out of the earth.
"Now find the potatoes," he said.
They all looked.
Then Sue saw them.
They were small.
But they were there.

They were on the part of the plant

that had been growing

under the ground.

"How small they are!" said Sue.

"They will grow bigger

all through the summer,"

said Mr. Bartilucci.

"You can still see the seed potato

that we planted."

"Who digs up the potatoes

when they are ready?"

asked one of the boys.

"A big machine digs them up

in September," said Mr. Bartilucci.

"Can we come then

to see how it works?"

asked the teacher.

"I am very busy then,"

said Mr. Bartilucci.

"But I guess you can come and watch.

I'll let you know when."

On the way home,

Sue asked her teacher,

"Why do new plants

grow from those pieces of potatoes

he plants?"

"Mr. Bartilucci told you,"

said the teacher.

"There are buds

in the eyes of the potato

that can grow into new plants.

When you get home,

look into the bag of potatoes

your mother has."

When Sue got home,

she ran into the kitchen.

She looked into the bag of potatoes.

47

"This one is growing

without being planted,"

she said to her mother.

"It is growing from the eye

of the potato."

Then she asked her mother

to cut the potato into four pieces.

"These," she said,

"are what the farmer plants."

In September,

Sue went back to school.

She was glad to have the same teacher.

Most of the children in the class

were the same too.

Sue asked, "When can we go to see

Mr. Bartilucci?"

"I already have a note from him.

We can take our trip to his farm

next Wednesday," said the teacher.

On Wednesday, the class went back

to the farm.

There was a big truck

in the middle of the field.

Next to it was a tractor

pulling a giant machine.

One of the children said,

"The potato plants look dead!"

"That's right," the teacher said.

"They are all brown

and dead-looking.

The children want to know

why the potato plants look dead,"

she said to Mr. Bartilucci.

"That is the way

they are supposed to look

when we dig them,"

said Mr. Bartilucci.

"When the tops die,

we know the potatoes

under the ground are ready.

"Now move to one side."

The teacher and the class

moved away from the machines.

Mr. Bartilucci started the tractor

that pulled the giant machine.

Mr. Bartilucci's wife started

the truck that went alongside.

The giant machine dug

two rows of potatoes at a time.

Potatoes started to tumble up

a moving chain belt on the machine.

Dirt and dead vines fell through

to the ground.

But the potatoes stayed on the belt.

Then they fell into the truck.

After a few minutes, Mrs. Bartilucci

stopped the truck.

Mr. Bartilucci climbed down

from the tractor.

"Here," he said to Sue,

"dig up a plant now."

Sue dug all around a potato plant.

Mr. Bartilucci helped her.

When they were finished,

there were ten big potatoes

on the ground.

In the spring, the class

had seen tiny potatoes.

Now they were very big.

Mr. Bartilucci said to the teacher,

"My truck is full.

Follow me to the warehouse."

"Another warehouse!" said Sue.

The farmer got into the truck.

The children climbed into the bus.

They drove to a big building.

"Take the children inside,"

said Mr. Bartilucci to the teacher.

They saw a little door open

in the wall next to the truck.

Potatoes started to tumble

through the door

and onto a moving belt.

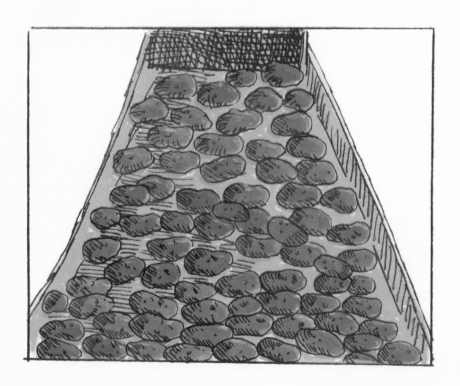

Then the potatoes

went through a machine

that washed and dried them.

Then they rolled down another belt.

At the end, they fell

into big bags.

"What happens to these bags?"

asked the teacher.

The man near the bags said,

"They go on a truck."

"I know where they go then,"

said Sue.

"They go to another warehouse.

Then they go on another truck.

Then they go to the store.

That is how the store

gets more potatoes!"